DISCOVER AMERICA

MISSISSIPPI

Jill Foran

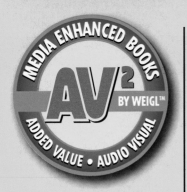

AV² provides enriched content that supplements and complements this book. Weigl's AV² books strive to create inspired learning and engage young minds in a total learning experience.

Your AV² Media Enhanced books come alive with...

Audio
Listen to sections of the book read aloud.

Key Words
Study vocabulary, and complete a matching word activity.

Video
Watch informative video clips.

Quizzes
Test your knowledge.

Go to **www.av2books.com**, and enter this book's unique code.

BOOK CODE

S272747

Embedded Weblinks
Gain additional information for research.

Slide Show
View images and captions, and prepare a presentation.

AV² by Weigl brings you media enhanced books that support active learning.

Try This!
Complete activities and hands-on experiments.

... and much, much more!

Published by AV² by Weigl
350 5th Avenue, 59th Floor
New York, NY 10118
Website: www.av2books.com

Library of Congress Cataloging-in-Publication Data
Names: Foran, Jill, author.
Title: Mississippi : the Magnolia State / Jill Foran.
Description: New York, NY : AV2 by Weigl, [2016] | Series: Discover America | Includes index.
Identifiers: LCCN 2015048021 (print) | LCCN 2015048325 (ebook) | ISBN 9781489648877 (hard cover : alk. paper) | ISBN 9781489648884 (soft cover : alk. paper) | ISBN 9781489648891 (Multi-User eBook)
Subjects: LCSH: Mississippi--Juvenile literature.
Classification: LCC F341.3 .F675 2016 (print) | LCC F341.3 (ebook) | DDC 976.2--dc23
LC record available at http://lccn.loc.gov/2015048021

Printed in the United States of America, in Brainerd, Minnesota
1 2 3 4 5 6 7 8 9 20 19 18 17 16

042016
220416

Project Coordinator Heather Kissock
Art Director Terry Paulhus

Photo Credits
Every reasonable effort has been made to trace ownership and to obtain permission to reprint copyright material. The publisher would be pleased to have any errors or omissions brought to their attention so that they may be corrected in subsequent printings. The publisher acknowledges Getty Images, Corbis Images, and Alamy as its primary image suppliers for this title.

MISSISSIPPI

Contents

STATE TREE
Magnolia

STATE BIRD
Mockingbird

STATE FLAG
Mississippi

STATE FLOWER
Magnolia

STATE ANIMAL
White-tailed Deer

STATE SEAL
Mississippi

Nickname
The Magnolia State

Motto
Virtute et Armis
(By Valor and Arms)

Song
"Go, Mississippi" by Houston
Davis

Population
(2014 Census) 2,994,079
Ranked 31st state

Entered the Union
December 10, 1817, as the 20th state

Capital
Jackson

Discover Mississippi

Mississippi is located in the Deep South of the United States. It is named after the Mississippi River, which forms most of its western border. The Mississippi River runs through most of the central United States and empties into the Gulf of Mexico. This great river is responsible for much of Mississippi's rich soil and **fertile** land.

Four other southern states border Mississippi. Tennessee lies to the north, Alabama to the east, Arkansas to the west, and Louisiana to the west and south. The Gulf of Mexico borders southeastern Mississippi. This strip of land is known as the Gulf Coast.

The history and heritage of Mississippi is on full display for visitors to the state. The Natchez Parkway is a 444-mile road where guests can drive, hike, bike, or horseback ride through more than 8,000 years of North American history. Civil War enthusiasts will find historical museums and exhibits in Vicksburg, Port Gibston, and Natchez. Tourists can also visit **plantation** homes that have been preserved throughout the state.

Modern Mississippi is a state full of culture, music, and regional food. The state has a few large cities, but the variety of small cities gives the state its charm. The Gulf Coast is a popular tourist destination and Mississippi's beaches offer more than 60 miles of shoreline. These beaches are perfect for families as the waves are small due to a string of barrier islands just offshore. The Gulf Coast features outdoor activities, like paddle boarding, bird watching, and fishing.

The Land

Natchez, Mississippi, which was settled in 1716, is the **oldest permanent settlement** on the Mississippi River.

Forests make up almost **65 percent** of the Mississippi landscape.

Jackson, Mississippi, was named after President Andrew Jackson. A statue of him stands in front of Jackson's city hall.

By the time of the Civil War, there were more than 430,000 African American slaves living in Mississippi.

Beginnings

The first explorers to Mississippi were French, Spanish, and British. Settlement first began along the Gulf Coast. In 1716, the French started colonizing along the Mississippi River. Fort Rosalie, which would later become Natchez, was a major trading post.

Mississippi is probably best known for its cotton history. During the 1800s, many settlers became rich from growing cotton. As a result, the state became known as King Cotton.

Slavery was very much a part of the Deep South during this time. African American slaves performed the backbreaking work of planting and picking the cotton. When states in the North threatened to end or at least limit slavery, 11 Southern states, including Mississippi, seceded from, or left, the Union in 1860 and 1861. They formed the Confederate States of America. The Civil War began in 1861 between the Confederacy and the Union. The Union victory in 1865 marked the end of slavery in the United States.

Even after the Civil War, African Americans continued to suffer as a result of racial **segregation**. Not until the **civil rights movement** of the 1950s and 1960s did conditions begin to improve. During that time, the people of Mississippi played an important part in the fight for African American rights.

Where is MISSISSIPPI?

The winding Mississippi River forms most of the western border of the state, while the Pearl River provides the southwestern border. Except for a small portion of the northeastern corner where the Tennessee River separates Mississippi from Alabama, the state's northern and eastern borders are straight lines. The southeastern border is formed from the **bayous** and inlets of the Gulf of Mexico.

ARKANSAS

LOUISIANA

United States Map

Mississippi

Alaska   Hawai'i

MAP LEGEND

- ■ Mississippi
- ☆ Capital City
- ● Major City
- ▲ Natchez Historical Park
- ╲ Yazoo River
- □ Bordering States
- □ Water

N

SCALE   0   50 miles

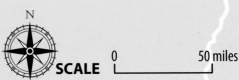

1 Jackson

Named after President Andrew Jackson, the city of Jackson is the largest urban area in Mississippi. In addition to being the capital, Jackson is home to cultural events ranging from blues music concerts to ballet performances. Home to Mississippi's state legislature, the latest capitol is the third capitol building erected in Jackson.

2 Hattiesburg

Hattiesburg is nicknamed Hub City because railroads used to intersect there. Today, many of those old railroad lines have been reclaimed and turned into biking paths. The city is a bustling center of southern culture and played a major role in the civil rights movement of the 1960s.

Yazoo River

MISSISSIPPI

ALABAMA

1

⭐ Jackson

3

2

Hattiesburg

Gulf of Mexico

3 Natchez Historical Park

The Natchez National Historical Park is a national park that reveals the **antebellum** history of the city of Natchez. The park includes the home of William Johnson, a free African American businessman, and Melrose, a former plantation, where visitors can enjoy tours and exhibits.

4 Yazoo River

The Yazoo River runs parallel to the larger Mississippi River for 190 miles. A series of **levees** protect surrounding areas from flooding. The river's delta is considered the birthplace of the blues, and it is also a prime location for growing cotton.

Land Features

The Mississippi **Alluvial** Plain covers the western edge of the state. It is made up of broad, flat lowlands that were once the **floodplains** of the Mississippi River. The Gulf Coastal Plain makes up the rest of the state. It has hills, stretches of marshy land, prairies, pinewoods, and plains. Offshore are several sandy islands, which are popular with explorers, nature lovers, and sunbathers.

Soil **erosion** is a problem in Mississippi. The wind and weather have worn away the fertile upper part of the soil in some areas. In other areas, erosion has formed **gullies**. Over the years, cotton farming has decreased much of the land's fertility. To prevent further soil erosion and restore fertility to the soil, large areas of eroded land have been planted with trees or turned into pasture.

Gulf Coast Islands

The Gulf Islands National Seashore extends along the Gulf of Mexico from Mississippi to Florida. White quartz sand covers the islands, as well as salt marshes, dunes, and low shrubs.

Swamps

Many Mississippi swamps are untouched by development. They provide a habitat for species that are in danger of dying out, such as the American alligator and wood stork. Swamps can also store water from heavy rainstorms and help control floods.

Mississippi River

The Mississippi River curves and winds along the state's western edge. White pelicans and other birds flock to feed in its slow-moving water.

Prairie

The Black Belt is part of the eastern Gulf Coastal Plain. This narrow region runs from Tennessee through Mississippi to Alabama. Fertile soil covers part of the Black Belt.

Climate

Mississippi's climate is warm and moist. The summers are hot and humid, with temperatures in July averaging about 90° Fahrenheit. However, summer temperatures in Mississippi can top 110°F. The highest temperature recorded was 115°F in Holly Springs on July 29, 1930. Hurricanes sometimes sweep up from the Gulf Coast in the late summer.

Winters in Mississippi are mild, with abundant rainfall and an average temperature of about 43°F. Temperatures can drop below freezing, however. A temperature of –19°F was recorded at Corinth on January 30, 1966.

Average Annual Precipitation Across Mississippi

Cities in different parts of Mississippi typically receive different amounts of rainfall over the course of a year. Why might Biloxi get as much precipitation as it does in a year?

LEGEND
Average Annual Precipitation (in inches) 1961–1990

200 – 100.1

100 – 25.1

25 – 5 and less

ARKANSAS

LOUISIANA

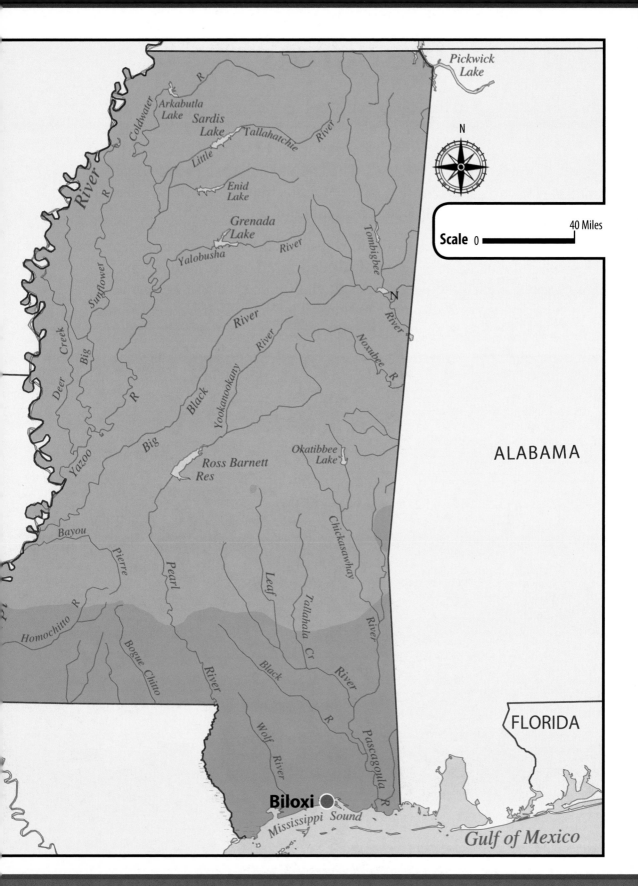

Pickwick
Lake

Coldwater

R

Arkabutla
Lake

Sardis
Lake

Little

Tallahatchie

River

River

Enid
Lake

Grenada
Lake

Yalobusha

River

Tombigbee

Sunflower

River

River

N

River

Noxubee

R

Big

R

Deer Creek

Black

Yookanookany

Big

Yazoo

Ross Barnett
Res

Okatibbee
Lake

N

Scale 0 ━━━━━━ 40 Miles

ALABAMA

Bayou

Pierre

Pearl

Leaf

Chickasawhay

Homochitto
R

Bogue Chitto

River

Black

Tallahala Cr

River

River

FLORIDA

Wolf

River

R

Pascagoula

Biloxi ●

R

Mississippi Sound

Gulf of Mexico

Nature's Resources

Fresh water and fertile soil are plentiful in Mississippi and are the state's most important natural resources. Mississippi's many rivers and lakes provide the state with large supplies of surface water, and numerous wells also dot the land. The lakes of Mississippi are not all natural. The largest lakes are a result of dams that were built to prevent river floods that would damage crops and homes.

The floodwaters of the past were also responsible for positive changes. The soil in the delta is made up of **silt** deposited on the land when the Mississippi River overflowed. This alluvial soil is excellent for growing crops, which is why cotton thrives there. The Black Belt, where the soil is mainly a rich black, is another fertile area.

The timber industry in Mississippi earns between $1.3 and $1.5 billion every year for the state.

Natural gas and petroleum are the primary mined natural resources. They are found in the southern part of the state. Clays used in industry as well as sand and gravel are mined there as well.

Another important natural resource in Mississippi is its forests. They provide wood for construction and paper products. Most of the state's timber comes from pine trees. Mississippi is one of the country's top producers of lumber.

While Mississippi is a natural gas-producing state, it consumes more natural gas than is produced.

Cotton is the third-highest money-making crop in Mississippi.

Vegetation

Mississippi is heavily forested. In the northern part of the state, the forests consist of tulip trees, sycamores, honey locusts, and many species of oaks and hickories. Swamp oaks, bald cypresses, and tupelos can be found in the forests of the delta. Many kinds of pines grow in the Piney Woods, which cover much of southern Mississippi. Pecan and magnolia trees grow throughout the state.

There was a time when nearly all of Mississippi was forested. When settlers arrived, they cut down the trees to create farmland. As time passed, swamps were drained, and levees were built to control flooding. Many more trees were cut down for the lumber industry.

Today, the state has a program of planting young trees to replace those cut down for their lumber. Much of Mississippi's abandoned farmland has been replanted with trees. Other efforts to preserve Mississippi's forests and wildlife include setting up state and national parks and funding wildlife and nature **preserves**.

Azaleas

Azaleas thrive in the shaded Mississippi forests and wetlands. Their trumpet-like flowers appear in early spring.

Bellflower

The bellflower is native to Mississippi. Its star-shaped flowers grow on top of 2-foot, hairy stems.

Water Tupelo

The water tupelo is also known as the cottongum, sourgum, swamp tupelo, tupelo-gum, and water-gum tree. It can grow from 80 to 100 feet tall, with a large swelling at its base. Its root system is often underwater.

Live Oak

The trunk of a live oak divides near the ground into long branches. The tops of a live oak's leaves are green and glossy, while the undersides are hairy and whitish. Ships were once built of its strong, heavy wood.

Wildlife

Foxes, raccoons, opossums, rabbits, squirrels, armadillos, and wild turkeys can all be found in Mississippi's forests. Alligators lurk in many of the state's swampy areas. They share these damp places with turtles and frogs. Since large quantities of land have been opened to farming and hunting, much of the big game that once roamed the forests has become very scarce. Wolves, cougars, and bison have all disappeared from Mississippi.

There are many types of fish in Mississippi. Catfish, bream, bass, and perch are found in the state's fresh waters. Shrimps, oysters, and saltwater fish live in the offshore waters of the Gulf of Mexico.

Wild Turkey

Wild turkeys can fly only short distances, less than 0.25 miles. They eat berries, nuts, seeds, insects, and sometimes frogs and lizards. Male wild turkeys are larger and more brightly colored than female turkeys.

Mississippi Gopher Frog

The Mississippi Gopher frog only lives around three ponds in southern Mississippi. This frog spends a lot of time in old stumps or in woodland burrows. The species relies on Mississippi's native longleaf pine ecosystem.

American Alligator

American alligators usually range from 6 to 12 feet long but can grow to 19 feet. They use their powerful tails to swim and to defend themselves. Both males and females hiss noisily, and males can also roar loudly.

Opossum

The Virginia opossum found in Mississippi is the only marsupial living north of Mexico in North America. Marsupials are animals with pouches to carry their young. About the size of a cat, opossums live in trees and eat insects, eggs, baby birds, fruit, and small mammals.

Economy

Vicksburg National Military Park

With its lines of cannons, the Confederate fortress at Vicksburg guarded the Mississippi River from Union attacks. When it fell, Union forces gained full control of the river.

Tourism

The sunny beaches of the Gulf Coast are lined with large hotels, fine restaurants, and many tourist attractions. Visitors can see what life may have been like in Mississippi before the Civil War by visiting the mansions in Vicksburg or Natchez. During the tourist season, dozens of local mansions are opened to the public in Natchez.

In Vicksburg, tourists can also visit the National Military Park. This park preserves one of the most important battlefields of the Civil War. Exhibits at the military park include replicas of soldiers' quarters and the caves in which civilians hid during the battle for Vicksburg.

Rock and Blues Heritage Museum

The museum honors the South's role in the history of rock and blues. Guests can experience artifacts from the 1920s to the 1970s. The site of the museum is thought to be where the first rock album was ever recorded.

Longwood Mansion

Longwood Mansion's unique eight-sided construction was begun in the 1860s but was halted due to the outbreak of the Civil War. While the outside is finished, only 9 of its 32 rooms are complete.

Biloxi Beaches

Biloxi attracts tourists with its white sand beaches as well as its casinos.

Cotton production generates about $600 million for the state each year.

Primary Industries

For more than a century before the U.S. joined World War II in 1941, agriculture dominated Mississippi's economy. Cotton was the main crop. After World War II, tractors, mechanical cotton pickers, and **combines** took the place of human laborers. Plantations, which had provided jobs for many families, quickly became mechanized. Today, cotton plantations require only a few people to operate the machines. Cotton is still a leading crop, along with soybeans, but it is less important to the economy than it once was.

In the 1960s, manufacturing surpassed agriculture as a source of income in Mississippi. The state produces a wide variety of goods, including clothing, processed foods, electronic equipment, lumber and wood products, and chemicals. Mississippi is also a leading producer of upholstered furniture.

Mississippi's **agriculture** industry employs about **30 percent** of its workforce.

Mississippi catches and sells more **catfish** than anywhere else in the world.

Value of Goods and Services (in Millions of Dollars)

Although Mississippi's economy once relied heavily on farming, especially on growing cotton, today the state is focusing on bringing more tourists to the area. Why are finance, insurance, and real estate important to the tourism industry?

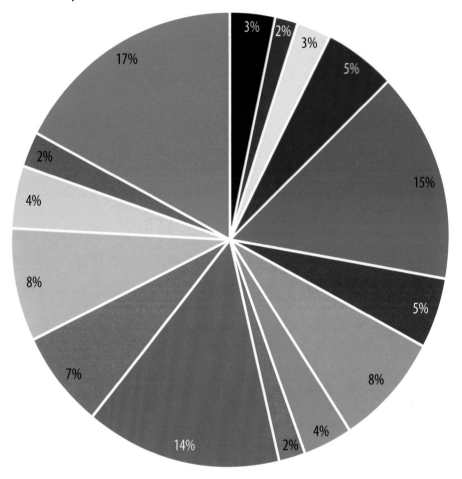

- Agriculture, forestry, fishing $3,519
- Mining $1,742
- Utilities $2,875
- Construction $5,331
- Manufacturing $15,864
- Wholesale trade $5,192
- Retail trade $8,328
- Transportation and warehousing $3,742
- Information $2,257
- Finance, Insurance, and Real Estate $15,157
- Professional and Business Services $7,221
- Education, Health Care, and Social Services ... $8,421
- Entertainment and Accommodations $4,657
- Other Services $2,510
- Government $17,936

Mississippi produces about 350 million pounds of catfish each year.

Goods and Services

Mississippi's farms not only produce cotton, corn, and soybeans, they also raise fish. Mississippi catfish are bred to be lighter and tastier than the catfish that grow in the state's streams and rivers. The Delta region leads the nation in farm-raised catfish production. Areas along the Gulf Coast are among the country's main suppliers of shrimp.

The leading processed-food products in Mississippi are meat products, baked goods, and seafood products. In 2009, Mississippi was the fifth-largest producer of broiler chickens in the nation. They are also one of the top three producers of oysters in the United States.

Mississippi has 15 ports along the Gulf Coast and the Mississippi River. The waters in Gulfport and Pascagoula are often crowded with oceangoing ships. Smaller boats travel up the Mississippi River to Natchez, Vicksburg, and Greenville. The Tennessee-Tombigbee Waterway, which opened in 1985, has become a chief shipping route in the east. It provides the state's growing industries with a quick and inexpensive route for shipping goods to ports along the Gulf Coast.

The hotels and resorts of the Gulf Coast provide many jobs for Mississippians. Casino gambling in Mississippi is legal only if it is done offshore, so floating casinos have been built. They draw people from all over North America and have given a big boost to Mississippi's economy. The tourist season for the Gulf Coast is mainly from May to August, but recently there has been a push to enjoy the coast year round, despite the colder temperatures in the winter.

The eastern oyster, a species of oyster native to the Gulf Coast, is popular in Mississippi. It is served at most local restaurants.

More than 300 million tons of cargo move up and down the Mississippi River each year.

Choctaw prophets, or priests, often dressed in ceremonial regalia. This Native American group worshiped the Sun.

The Grand Village of the Natchez Indians spans 128 acres. It features a reconstructed Natchez house and three prehistoric Native American mounds.

Native Americans

At least 2,000 years ago, the Mississippi region was populated by Native Americans who piled layers of dirt on top of big pits to form giant mounds. The Mound Builders were highly skilled in farming and architecture. Some mounds served as burial sites, while others were places of worship. Chiefs and priests lived on special mounds, and their houses or temples stood above the villages.

By 1500, the Mound Builders had largely disappeared, and three distinct Native American groups dominated the region. The Choctaw lived mostly in central and southern Mississippi, the Chickasaw controlled the northern part of the region, and the Natchez dominated the southwest. The Biloxi and Pascagoula people also lived in the southern part of the state. In 1540, when the first European explorers arrived in the Mississippi region, about 30,000 Native Americans were living there.

The Choctaw and Chickasaw are closely related. They have similar languages and traditions, and the two groups traded goods in the past. Chickasaw hunters gave hides to Choctaw farmers in exchange for corn.

The Natchez grew corns, beans, and squash and hunted animals in the lush forests. Probably starting in the 1300s, they built their main ceremonial mound at what is now the Grand Village of the Natchez Indians. The Natchez are known for their social caste system.

Exploring the Land

Hernando de Soto, a Spanish explorer, was the first European known to visit the Mississippi area. In 1540, de Soto and his army passed through the northern part of the region looking for gold. The Chickasaws resisted their invasion. Some of de Soto's soldiers had smallpox and other diseases that were new to North America. Native Americans had no **immunity** to these diseases, and as a result, many died. De Soto and his men left the region without finding any gold.

Timeline of Settlement

Early European Settlements

1682 René-Robert Cavelier, sieur de La Salle, travels down the Mississippi River to the Gulf of Mexico and claims the Mississippi region for France.

1673 French missionary Jacques Marquette and map maker Louis Jolliet reach Mississippi and explore as far south as present-day Rosedale before turning back.

1699 Pierre Le Moyne and his brother, Jean-Baptiste, found the first European settlement, at Fort Maurepas near today's Ocean Springs on the Gulf Coast.

1540–1541 The Spanish explorer Hernando de Soto is the first known European to enter Mississippi. In the spring of 1541, his group reaches the Mississippi River, a few miles south of present-day Memphis, Tennessee.

1716 The French establish Fort Rosalie, the beginning of the town of Natchez.

1719 French slave traders bring the first slaves to Mississippi from Jamaica, a Caribbean island.

Early Exploration

The next Europeans to enter the Mississippi region arrived more than 100 years later. In 1682, a French explorer named René-Robert Cavelier, sieur de La Salle, traveled down the Mississippi River to the Gulf of Mexico. He claimed the Mississippi region for France. In 1699, Pierre Le Moyne, sieur d'Iberville, established the first permanent settlement in the area, Fort Maurepas, on Biloxi Bay.

At first, the French got along with the Natchez people. When the French colony grew, disputes broke out. In 1729, the Natchez attacked Fort Rosalie, and the French fought back. By 1731, almost all of the Natchez had been killed or forced to leave.

Statehood and Civil War

1817 Mississippi becomes a state.

1861 Mississippi secedes from the United States and joins the Confederacy. The Civil War begins.

1798 The Mississippi Territory is established by the U.S. government.

1783 Most of Mississippi becomes part of the United States under the treaty ending the American Revolutionary War.

1763 The British gain control of Mississippi at the end of the French and Indian War.

1865 The Confederacy is defeated, and the Civil War ends.

Changes of Control

1871 Mississippi reenters the Union as a state.

In the 1720s, the Natchez raided the French because they treated the Native Americans unfairly.

The First Settlers

During the early 1700s, several thousand French settlers came to the Mississippi. They were lured by the promise of earning money quickly and easily by investing in the Mississippi Company. This business's task was to develop the vast French territories in the Mississippi River Valley.

The company quickly became very powerful in the French economy. However, it collapsed after just a few years. The small number of settlers who stayed in the region lived near the French forts. Many people were unwilling to come to the area because of the frequent warfare between the French and the British.

In 1763, the British defeated the French in the French and Indian War. Under the treaty that ended the war, France surrendered Mississippi to Great Britain. The treaty also gave the British control of the Spanish territory of Florida, which they divided into two. One of these, West Florida, included what is now southern Mississippi.

In the 1800s, cotton traveled north to textile mills via the Mississippi River. Some cotton was also shipped to Europe.

During the American Revolutionary War, the Spanish retook this territory from the British. At the end of the war in 1783, the British surrendered most of Mississippi to the United States. It was not until end of the 1700s and the beginning of the 1800s that all Spanish claims to southern Mississippi were ended and all of the present-day state was in U.S. hands.

During the late 1700s and early 1800s, thousands of settlers arrived from the more crowded U.S. states to the east. The mid-1800s saw Mississippi settlers using slave labor to make huge profits by growing cotton on plantations. Slavery continued in Mississippi until the Civil War ended.

Plantation homes became a symbol of the South. Today, visitors can tour many of the stately and iconic homes in Mississippi.

History Makers

Many notable Mississippians contributed to the development of their state and their country. They advocated for civil rights for all Americans, fighting against segregation and illegal hangings, as well as for voter rights. They also were business leaders and generous donors to charitable causes. Some even piloted spaceships and then ran the organizations that developed programs to further explore space.

Hiram R. Revels (1822–1901)

Hiram R. Revels was the first African American senator in U.S. history. He served from January 1870 to March 1871, completing the term of Jefferson Davis, who was the former president of the Confederacy. Revels advocated for the civil rights of African Americans, including the right to be educated in **desegregated** schools. He also argued that former members of the Confederacy should be allowed to vote.

Ida B. Wells (1862–1931)

Ida Wells was born into slavery in Holly Springs and began teaching at age 14. After writing several articles criticizing the education that African Americans received, she lost her job as a teacher and turned to newspaper editing and writing.

Medgar Evers (1925–1963)

Medgar Evers worked for the National Association for the Advancement of Colored People, a civil rights organization. He encouraged African Americans to vote. On June 12, 1963, Medgar Evers was shot to death in front of his home. His assassin was brought to trial twice in the 1960s but not convicted until 1994. The death of Evers made him a symbol of the civil rights movement.

Richard Truly (1937–)

Richard Truly piloted the Space Shuttle *Columbia*, the first spacecraft with a crew to be sent into space a second time. In 1983, he also commanded the *Challenger* during its first night mission. He ran the National Aeronautics and Space Administration from 1989 to 1992, the first former astronaut to head this space agency.

Oprah Winfrey (1954–)

One of the richest women in the world, Oprah Winfrey was born to a poor single mother. In 1985, she began hosting her own TV talk show. The *Oprah Winfrey Show* became the highest-rated talk show in U.S. history. Known for her generosity, she has given money to a number of charitable causes.

Culture

The Mississippi Daughters of the American Revolution is a local chapter of a national group that works to maintain historical culture.

According to Pew polling data, Mississippi is the most religious state in the U.S. Sixty percent of residents say they attend a religious service at least once a week.

The People Today

Mississippi is largely a rural state. Of the nearly 3 million people who live in Mississippi, about half live on farms or in small towns. In recent years, many Mississippians have moved to cities in search of jobs.

Most people in Mississippi with a European background have British, Irish, or Northern European heritage. Up until 1940, more than half of the people in Mississippi were African American. After 1940, many African Americans moved to cities in the northern states in search of job opportunities. Today, about 37 percent of Mississippi's population is African American.

Mississippi's population grew by 10.5 percent from 1990 to 2000 but only by 4.3 percent from 2000 to 2010.

Q What are some reasons for this change in population growth rate?

On top of the Mississippi state capitol dome is an 8-foot-tall bronze eagle.

State Government

Mississippi has had four constitutions. The first was adopted in 1817, when Mississippi became a state. It was replaced by a second constitution in 1832, and a third one in 1868, when changes had to be made after the Civil War. The current state constitution was adopted in 1890. Under the Mississippi constitution, the state government has three branches.

The legislative branch makes the laws. This branch consists of the Senate and the House of Representatives. There are 52 senators and 122 representatives. All are elected to four-year terms and may serve any number of terms.

The second branch is the executive, headed by the governor. Like other top officials in the executive branch, the governor is elected to a four-year term and may not serve for more than two terms. The executive branch ensures that the laws are carried out.

The judicial branch sees that the laws are obeyed. It consists of the courts and their judges, who are elected. The highest court in the state is the Supreme Court.

The rotunda in the capitol building is made of Italian white marble. The pillars were completed with New York black marble.

Phil Bryant has been Mississippi's governor since 2012. He is the 63rd governor of the state.

Mississippi's state song is called
"Go, Mississippi."

States may sing their songs of praise

With waving flags and hip-hoo-rays,

Let cymbals crash and let bells ring

'Cause here's one song
I'm proud to sing.

Go, Mississippi, keep rolling along,

Go, Mississippi, you cannot
go wrong,

Go, Mississippi, we're singing your
song, M-I-S-S-I-S-S-I-P-P-I

Go, Mississippi, you're on the
right track,

Go, Mississippi, and this is a fact,

Go, Mississippi, you'll never look
back, M-I-S-S-I-S-S-I-P-P-I

* excerpted

Each March and October, the Mississippi Blues Fest in Greenwood celebrates the culture of blues music in the Mississippi Delta.

Celebrating Culture

There is a wide range of cultures in Mississippi. Many of these cultures can be seen particularly in the southern part of the state, both in the buildings and in the local customs. French, Spanish, British, Latin American, and African American traditions are especially evident.

African American culture is very strong throughout Mississippi. Each year, the state holds celebrations honoring African American achievements, including the civil rights movement. African American culture can be seen in everything from literature to food.

It also has had a strong influence on music. Blues music originated in the cotton fields of the Mississippi Delta. Today, the blues remains one of the most important types of music in Mississippi. Well-known blues musicians from the state include Bo Diddley, John Lee Hooker, Muddy Waters, and B.B. King. The Delta Blues Festival, held each fall in Greenville, honors well-known blues musicians and showcases new ones.

The Choctaw celebrate their history during the Choctaw Indian Fair, which is held once a year in the summer. The fair allows the Choctaw to exhibit their rich cultural past and celebrate with friends and family. The Choctaw are the state's only federally recognized Native American group.

Mardi Gras festivities and parades are celebrated along the coast in January or February. Mardi Gras means "Fat Tuesday" in French. It is traditionally celebrated before the Christian religious season of **Lent**.

The Choctaw Indian Fair has been a celebration of culture each July for more than 65 years.

The main Mardi Gras events in Mississippi cities are parades featuring elaborately decorated floats. Bystanders can catch treasures, such as beaded necklaces, being thrown from the floats.

Elvis Presley was born in Tupelo, Mississippi, in 1935.

Arts and Entertainment

Musicians from Mississippi have given the United States some of its most distinctive music. Perhaps the most celebrated Mississippi entertainer is Elvis Presley. He is well-known for popularizing rock and roll in the 1950s. His music combined country and western with rhythm and blues to create a truly unique sound. He became one of the most successful entertainers of his time, and his music is still popular today.

Jimmie Rodgers is often regarded as the Father of Country Music. Rodgers melded yodeling, steel guitars, and blues, cowboy, and hobo songs with country music, developing a sound called "blue yodeling." Rodgers was one of the first people inducted into the Country Music Hall of Fame.

Blues legend **Muddy Waters** was inducted into the **Rock and Roll Hall of Fame** in 1987.

Mississippi-born author **William Faulkner** won the **Nobel Prize for Literature** in 1949.

Some of Mississippi's most popular festivals celebrate the catfish and shrimp industries. The Shrimp Festival at Biloxi is held each spring at the beginning of the shrimping season. It includes dances, parades, and the crowning of a Shrimp Queen. The World Catfish Festival in Belzoni crowns Miss Catfish.

Museums and art galleries throughout Mississippi celebrate the state's culture and history. The major art gallery is the Mississippi Museum of Art in Jackson, but there are also many smaller galleries throughout the state. Tourists often make a special trip to Ocean Springs to see the art of Walter Anderson, the well-known Gulf Coast painter.

Known as "The Singing Brakeman," Jimmie Rodgers was born in Meridian, Mississippi, in 1897.

The Ohr-O'Keefe Museum of Art works to preserve and celebrate the work of Biloxi potter George E. Ohr.

OHR-O'KEEFE MUSEUM OF ART
NOW OPEN

Freshwater fishing is a major pastime in Mississippi, with more than 4,000 miles of streams and about 280,000 acres of lakes and reservoirs.

Sports and Recreation

Mississippi's many rivers and lakes provide plenty of opportunities for water-skiing, swimming, sailing, and fishing. The Tennessee-Tombigbee Waterway is lined with beaches, campgrounds, and docks for boats. Miles of sandy beaches along the Gulf Coast are also great for water sports, sunbathing, shell hunting, and other beach activities. State and national parks provide hikers and cyclists with many exciting trails to explore. Some of the most thrilling outdoor adventures can be found on the Gulf Islands National Seashore. The National Seashore preserves four islands off the eastern Mississippi coast.

Completely isolated, Horn Island is a preferred spot for the adventurous. In fact, the only way to get to Horn Island is by private boat. The island itself is a 3,650-acre strip of wilderness with forests, lagoons, and miles of deserted beaches.

The *LARGEST FOOTBALL STADIUM* in Mississippi is Davis-Wade Stadium with a capacity of more than *61,000 PEOPLE*.

In 2010, **Jerry Rice** of Crawford was inducted into the Pro Football Hall of Fame. Rice won three Super Bowls with the San Francisco 49ers.

A number of great athletes have come from Mississippi. The Mississippi Sports Hall of Fame recognizes many of them. Its displays include tributes to football greats Brett Favre and Jerry Rice. College football and basketball are also popular in Mississippi. Stickball is an ancient sport similar to lacrosse that is still played on the Choctaw Reservation. In centuries past, stickball games involved hundreds of players. Today, spectators can watch a stickball competition during the annual Choctaw Indian Fair.

Camping and boating are popular activities on Horn Island.

The University of Mississippi's football team won one national title, in 1955.

Get To Know
MISSISSIPPI

The Mississippi Petrified Forest is made up of giant fossilized trees and logs that date back 36 million years.

EDWARDS, MISSISSIPPI, IS THE HOME OF THE WORLD'S ONLY CACTUS PLANTATION.

Leontyne Price, of Laurel, Mississippi, was the first African American to achieve stardom in opera.

Mississippians are sometimes called **Mudcats**, after the freshwater **catfish** that live in the state.

Barq's Root Beer
WAS INVENTED IN BILOXI, MISSISSIPPI, IN 1898 BY EDWARD ADOLF BARQ, SR.

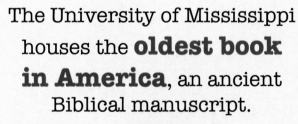

Biloxi's beach is the longest artificial beach in the world.

The University of Mississippi houses the **oldest book in America**, an ancient Biblical manuscript.

Brain Teasers

What have you learned about Mississippi after reading this book? Test your knowledge by answering these questions. All of the information can be found in the text you just read. The answers are provided below for easy reference.

1 What river forms most of Mississippi's western border?

2 What is Mississippi's nickname?

3 What was Mississippi's biggest crop in the 1800s?

4 What were the three main Native American groups living in the Mississippi area when Europeans arrived?

5 What kind of fish are bred in Mississippi's Delta region?

6 Which Mississippian was the first African American senator in U.S. history?

7 How many constitutions has Mississippi had?

8 What type of music was born in the Delta region?

ANSWER KEY
1. Mississippi River 2. The Magnolia State 3. Cotton 4. Choctaw, Chickasaws, and Natchez 5. Catfish 6. Hiram R. Revels 7. Four 8. Blues

Key Words

alluvial: consisting of deposits of clay or sand left by flowing water

antebellum: existing before a war

bayous: marshy outlets of a lake or river

civil rights movement: the struggle in the 1950s and 1960s to provide racial equality for African Americans

combines: harvesting machines that cut down crops

desegregated: ended legal separations and restrictions based on race

erosion: the wearing away of rock and soil

fertile: producing abundant plants or crops

floodplains: low-lying land located near rivers and subject to flooding

gullies: small valleys

immunity: natural defenses

Lent: in the Christian religion, the eight weeks before Easter; typically a period of fasting

levees: walls of stone or earth built to prevent the overflow of a river

Mardi Gras: a festival whose name means "Fat Tuesday" in French, celebrated on the final Tuesday before Christian Lent

plantation: large estate or farm on which crops such as cotton are grown

preserves: a place where animals and plants are protected in nature

segregation: the forced separation of races and restrictions based on race

silt: fine sand, clay, or other material carried by running water and deposited on land

Index

Log on to www.av2books.com

AV² by Weigl brings you media enhanced books that support active learning. Go to www.av2books.com, and enter the special code found on page 2 of this book. You will gain access to enriched and enhanced content that supplements and complements this book. Content includes video, audio, weblinks, quizzes, a slide show, and activities.

AV² Online Navigation

Audio
Listen to sections of the book read aloud.

Video
Watch informative video clips.

Embedded Weblinks
Gain additional information for research.

Try This!
Complete activities and hands-on experiments.

Book Pages
AV² pages directly correspond to pages in the book.

Key Words
Study vocabulary, and complete a matching word activity.

Quizzes
Test your knowledge.

Slide Show
View images and captions, and prepare a presentation.

AV² was built to bridge the gap between print and digital. We encourage you to tell us what you like and what you want to see in the future.

Sign up to be an AV² Ambassador at www.av2books.com/ambassador.